How to Overcome
Hopelessness and Despair

H.E. Metropolitan Youssef

ST MARY & MOSES ABBEY PRESS

How to Overcome Hopelessness and Despair

By Metropolitan Youssef

Designed & Published by:
St. Mary & St. Moses Abbey Press
101 S Vista Dr, Sandia, TX 78383
stmabbeypress.com

CONTENTS

INTRODUCTION

A person may feel despair when he goes through a difficult trial, an instance of failure, or when he hears bad news. He loses his joy and peace and enters into a cycle of unhappiness and hopelessness, which could lead to more failure during that time. Failure brings forth frustration and feeling down, and the cycle continues. And this cycle may continue to the point of developing a mental illness, like depression.

Through one of the amazing figures of the Holy Bible, Nehemiah, one can contemplate how to overcome frustration, failure, hopelessness, despair, and feeling down. We see how he turned it into success, for Nehemiah's motto was: "The God of heaven Himself will prosper us; therefore we His servants will arise and build" (Nehemiah 2:20). We will first discuss the reasons that may lead to feeling down, and second, how to deal with feeling down and frustrated.

1

REASONS THAT LEAD TO FEELING DOWN

1. Reasons that have to do with the person himself

a. <u>Making a wrong decision</u>. There are natural consequences that a person has to deal with after making a wrong decision that may cause him to feel down. For example, a person decided to emigrate but did not do proper research before taking the step. He did not consider what work he will do nor how he will live and acclimate but traveled anyway. When he arrived to the new country, he realized that things are not as he imagined them, but are going from bad to worse, and he begins to feel down and frustrated. He cannot undo his decision because he sold his house, left his job, and is afraid of what people will say when they see that he failed at taking this step. And if he stays in the new country, he will not be able to find stability, which can lead to despair

b. <u>Acting irresponsibly</u>. A worker who lashes out on his superior in a moment of anger, or a student who challenges his professor will suffer the consequences that may impact their future, all due to that irresponsible action. He might get fired or be unable to continue his education at that institution. He may feel down and frustrated as things worsen day by day.

c. <u>Bad habits</u>. A young man may start smoking, drinking, or using drugs. These activities begin as a sort of joke, something for pleasure, and the person is convinced that at any point he can quit using the substances. But when he tries, he finds that he is unable to stay away, which may lead him to feel down and frustrated.

d. <u>Defeating thoughts</u>. A person may not have self-confidence, and a feeling of failure begins to form inside him, letting him believe that he is not able to succeed at anything in his life. He may struggle with low self-esteem and be convinced that he is good for nothing. This can surely lead to despair.

2. Reasons that have to do with others:

a. <u>Destructive criticism</u>. There are parents who criticize their children for everything and never offer them encouraging words, saying that they are failures and will never succeed at anything, etc. Soon enough, these children will feel that they are of no use and that it is impossible to please their parents or for them to say anything encouraging, so they begin to despair.

b. <u>Persecution</u>. An example of persecution can be an employee who is working in honesty and doing his best to get his work done in the fear of God, but his superior still takes away from him any reward or promotion and goes as far as to criticize him. This worker may start to feel down after a while.

3. Natural reasons:

a. <u>Illness</u>. A person can fall into a difficult illness, making him suffer emotionally. Additionally, a father who has a child who suffers from a harsh illness or disability, suffers every time he sees his child, and therefore feels frustrated and down.

b. <u>Financial circumstances that the world is undergoing or that the family is struggling with</u>. For example, there is a person who works more than one job but his income does not cover the basic necessities, which can lead to some form of despair.

c. <u>Going through natural disasters and their difficult consequences can cause someone to feel down</u>.

Nehemiah received news that may have caused him to feel defeated. The Israelites were held captive, and he was one of them. He was hired to be the cupbearer for the king, which was an important job because the life of the king was in between his hands. It would not have been possible for someone to obtain this role if he was not trustworthy.

As he worked, many of the people who were still in Jerusalem and were not taken into captivity came to him. When he asked them about the people who were not in captivity, and about Jerusalem, they told him, "The survivors who are left from the captivity in the province are there in great distress and reproach. "The wall of Jerusalem is also broken down, and its gates are burned with fire" (Nehemiah 1:3). This was bad news for Nehemiah without a doubt, for Jerusalem was the city of the Great King, wherein is the Temple, the city that people loved and traveled to in order to worship God. The psalm says, "If I forget you, O Jerusalem, let my right hand forget its skill! If I do not remember you, let my tongue cling to the roof of my mouth—If I do not exalt Jerusalem above my chief joy" (Psalm 137:5–6). And when the captives were asked to sing praises to God, they would respond, "How shall we sing the Lord's song in a foreign land?" (Psalm 137:4). Nehemiah heard that those in Jerusalem were feeling down and defeated, for they were experiencing an evil time filled with shame, and Jerusalem's walls were destroyed. We all may go through tough times like these and feel hopeless.

This is similar to what happened with Saint Paul the Apostle, who went through a difficult trial. He described it in 2 Corinthians, "For we do not want you to be ignorant, brethren, of our trouble which came to us in Asia: that we were burdened beyond measure, above strength, so that we despaired even of life" (2 Corinthians 1:8). Let us imagine St. Paul, who said, "For if we live, we live to the Lord; and if we die, we die to the Lord. Therefore, whether we live or die, we are the Lord's" (Romans 14:8). And, "For to me, to live is Christ, and to die is gain" (Philippians 1:21). He is also the one who said, "For I am hard-pressed between the two, having a desire to depart and be with Christ, which is far better" (Philippians 1:23). Saint Paul was not afraid of death, but when he said "we were burdened beyond measure, above strength, so that we despaired even of life," it was clear that he had reached a deep sadness.

We all go through situations that strike us with deep sadness, and many times we do not have a hand in changing the circumstances, such as in times of sickness. Although we cannot control the reasons for sadness, we can control our reaction. Even though I cannot control the source of what troubles me, I can deal with the situation and be proactive.

> "Those who wish to acquire goodness and have the fear of God in their hearts, if they stumble or fall do not despair, but quickly rise with spiritual energy and more attention to good works."
>
> — Abba Moses the Strong —

2

DEALING WITH DESPAIR

How did Nehemiah and Paul the Apostle and other men of prayer, who were mentioned in chapter 11 of the Epistle to the Hebrews, deal with despair?

1. It is important for us to take whatever situation is causing sadness and deliver it up in prayer. The circumstance is bigger than me and I must share it with God and ask Him for the solution. This is what Nehemiah did when he heard the news about Jerusalem, he said, "So it was, when I heard these words, that I sat down and wept, and mourned for many days; I was fasting and praying before the God of heaven" (Nehemiah 1:4).

   He began by expressing his emotions through crying, then acknowledged that the situation is bigger than him and God needs to intervene. We can do nothing alone, without God: "for without Me you can do nothing" (John 15:5), how much more, then, is it difficult to act in severe situations that cause despair?

Nehemiah was a man of prayer. Scholars of the book of Nehemiah saw that Nehemiah utilized all forms of prayer. He prayed through ritual prayer when Ezra the scribe gathered the people and he read from the books of Moses and the law, and they celebrated the ritual services. He also prayed a personal prayer, an example of which is the prayer that is recorded in Chapter 1 of the book of Nehemiah. He also used what we call the arrow prayer when the king spoke to him in Chapter 2 and asked him, "What do you request?" to which Nehemiah responds, "So I prayed to the God of heaven. And I said to the king ..." (Nehemiah 2:4-5). This prayer took him only seconds before he answered the king, for he knew that success comes from God: "The God of heaven Himself will prosper us" (Nehemiah 2:20). The person who wishes to overcome despair cannot do so without prayer.

In the story of Hannah, the mother of Samuel, she could not have any children, causing her deep sadness along with the tormens from her husband's other wife. She complained to her husband, and he tried to comfort her saying, "Am I not better to you than ten sons?" (1 Samuel 1:8). But these words did not comfort her, and she resorted to prayer, which led her to victory over despair. After she prayed, she faced a difficult situation, where Eli the priest met her and thought she was drunk because she was praying in her heart, moving her lips while her voice was not heard. He said to her, "How long will you be drunk? Put your wine away from you!" (1 Samuel 1:14). Though her husband's wife and Eli the priest said harsh words to her, the power of prayer was much greater. Prayer granted Hannah power that did not allow the priest's harsh words to bother her. Rather, she responded to him saying, "No, my lord, I am a woman of sorrowful spirit. I have drunk neither wine nor intoxicating drink, but have poured out my soul before the Lord. Do not consider your maidservant a wicked woman, for out of the abundance of my complaint and grief I have spoken until now" (1 Samuel 1:15–16). And the Holy Bible then provides us a beautiful verse: "So the woman went her way and ate, and her face was no longer sad" (1 Samuel 1:18). Before, she had refused food and was depressed and feeling hopeless, but after she prayed, the power of prayer helped her to sustain hearing the harsh words and to be victorious over despair. She returned to her home and ate as a joyful person, and her face was no longer sad. All signs of failure and despair had left her face.

Prayer is an essential weapon to have victory over despair. Sometimes when man feels hopeless and in despair, he blames God in his prayer and is angry with God and asks God, "Why did You do this? Why did You leave me in this trial?" But when Nehemiah prayed, he confessed his sins and the sins of the people, saying, "Please let Your ear be attentive and Your eyes open, that You may hear the prayer of Your servant which I pray before You now, day and night, for the children of Israel Your servants, and confess the sins of the children of Israel which we have sinned against You. Both my father's house and I have sinned. We have acted very corruptly against You, and have not kept the commandments, the statutes, nor the ordinances which You commanded Your servant Moses" (Nehemiah 1:6–7).

Nehemiah was telling God that the trial they were going through was because of their own sins, and was telling God that He is holy, good, and just in His ways, but that they as a people did not walk in the ways of God that He gave them under the laws of Moses. Nehemiah did not complain or grumble or point the blame toward God, but instead confessed the goodness of the Lord: "I pray, Lord God of heaven, O great and awesome God, You who keep Your covenant and mercy with those who love You and observe Your commandments" (Nehemiah 1:5). Nehemiah asked for God's help with faith, as the Holy Bible says, "But let him ask in faith, with no doubting, for he who doubts is like a wave of the sea driven and tossed by the wind. For let not that man suppose that he will receive anything from the Lord" (James 1:6–7). For that reason Nehemiah said with confidence, "Now these are Your servants and Your people, whom You have redeemed by Your great power, and by Your strong hand. O Lord, I pray, please let Your ear be attentive to the prayer of Your servant, and to the prayer of Your servants who desire to fear Your name; and let Your servant prosper this day, I pray, and grant him mercy in the sight of this man" (Nehemiah 1:10–11). Nehemiah asked with faith and confidence for God to grant them success and help. And it is clear here that he not only prayed, but put in place a practical plan to follow because he said, "Let Your servant prosper this day, I pray, and grant him mercy in the sight of this man." For there to be success, there needs to be a human effort along with God's. The human side is what man is capable of doing, and God's side contains what man cannot do.

The first and most important thing in facing despair and failure, then, is praying with faith and confidence. During prayer we must remember God's goodness, confess our sins and purify ourselves, and then lay out a plan for God to bless.

2. Nehemiah was a practical man: "therefore we His servants will arise and build" (Nehemiah 2:20). There are people who ask God for help but do not do their role. Nehemiah had a big and important job in the king's palace as a cupbearer; he could have cried for a little and prayed for God's mercy and that would have been the end of the matter; rather, Nehemiah's life changed after hearing this news. He felt a duty and a responsibility to work and make a plan to better Jerusalem so that it may return to its first state and end its failure and despair. Nehemiah did not surrender to any spirit of defeat. There was internal resistance against him from the people of Israel as well as external resistance from people such as Sanballat the Horonite, Tobiah the Ammonite, and Geshem the Arabian. But

Nehemiah did not allow their resistance to stand in the way of his work.

There is a beautiful story in the Paradise of the Fathers that describes a group of thieves who entered a monastery in order to steal from it while the monks were praying at the same time. One of the monks went to the head of the monastery and told him that there were thieves stealing from the monastery. The elder told the monk, "We are doing our work—that is, praise and prayer—and they are doing their work. Let us not allow the matter to hinder our work and steal from us the blessing." So Nehemiah was a practical man, and if we wish to defeat feelings of failure and despair, we must say what he said: "Therefore we His servants will arise and build." We must do what we need to do, while seeking the help of God. If a person wishes to overcome an evil habit like smoking or drinking, he must exert effort and do what he needs to do and seek professional help if the matter calls for it, while asking that God grant him success. The Holy Bible says, "You have not yet resisted to bloodshed, striving against sin" (Hebrews 12:4). He who resists until bloodshed with strength and courage while asking God's help will indeed defeat failure and despair.

"Beware of despairing of yourself,
for you were commanded to trust in God
and not in yourself."

— Saint Augustine —

3. In order to defeat failure and despair one must have faith that God will grant us success: "The God of heaven Himself will prosper us; therefore we His servants will arise and build." When Saint Paul was going through a difficult trial that made him say, "We were burdened beyond measure, above strength, so that we despaired even of life. Yes, we had the sentence of death in ourselves," what made him victorious was his faith. Let us contemplate on what he said and what his thinking was. He said, "we despaired even of life" and "had the sentence of death in ourselves." Can God do anything to one who is dead? God can indeed raise the dead! Even if I reach a point of despair in my life that is so severe and I am like the dead, I should still never lose my hope nor let the despair crawl into my heart. But what I need in this life is to depend on God who

raises the dead, and therefore despair will not enter into my heart, because God is able to deliver me even from death. This is what Saint Paul said, "For we do not want you to be ignorant, brethren, of our trouble which came to us in Asia: that we were burdened beyond measure, above strength, so that we despaired even of life. Yes, we had the sentence of death in ourselves, that we should not trust in ourselves but in God who raises the dead, who delivered us from so great a death, and does deliver us; in whom we trust that He will still deliver us" (2 Corinthians 1:8–10). Saint Paul overcame failure and despair by his faith in God and his confidence that God delivered, is delivering, and will deliver us from death.

Faith and confidence ought to be present in us so that we do not rely on ourselves. If Saint Paul was relying on himself, he would have had the right to feel failure and defeat, but his confidence was in God who shuts the mouths of lions, quenches the power of fire, and raises Lazarus from his tomb even after four days.

This faith made Nehemiah plan and stand before God to explain to Him the situation, in addition to asking the king for letters to take for the governors of the region beyond the river, and for timber, and for many other things.

"Do not despair and do not worry, God searches for the salvation of sinners who are able and sinners who are not able, for He pities you and grants you repentance and strengthens you."

— His Holiness Pope Shenouda III —

4. It is important to pay attention to the positives and not focus on the negatives. For man to be able to defeat failure and despair, he must not give attention to the negatives or allow them to change his thinking. Oftentimes, a person may become depressed when he becomes passive and pays lots of attention to destructive criticism that may emotionally harm him. Nehemiah faced this with great strength and did not care as he said, "and all of them conspired together to come and attack Jerusalem and create confusion" (Nehemiah 4:8).

What did Nehemiah do? He said in the next verse, "Nevertheless we made our prayer to our God, and because of them we set a watch against them day and night" (Nehemiah 4:9). He put guards in place so that the people would not hear this negativity and be affected by it. The more man avoids what is negative, the more he is able to resist the spirit of despair. The Holy Bible tells us, "Sanballat and Geshem sent to me, saying, 'Come, let us meet together among the villages in the plain of Ono.' But they thought to do me harm. So I sent messengers to them, saying, 'I am doing a great work, so that I cannot come down. Why should the work cease while I leave it and go down to you?' But they sent me this message four times, and I answered them in the same manner" (Nehemiah 6:2–4). Sanballat and Geshem nagged Nehemiah, but he was persistent to not listen to destructive criticism or to their negative matters, and at the same time persisted in his positive work.

5. It is important to maintain physical health. Nehemiah appreciated how important it was to maintain physical health as a talent given from God to overcome despair as Saint Paul said: "For no one ever hated his own flesh, but nourishes and cherishes it" (Ephesians 5:29). Sometimes when a man feels down, he neglects himself and either eats too little or too much, and may not keep

a healthy sleep schedule, and then enters a stage that may lead to depression.

Maintaining physical health as a talent helps man to overcome feelings of defeat and despair, which we read about in Nehemiah, "Then Judah said, 'The strength of the laborers is failing, and there is so much rubbish that we are not able to build the wall'" (Nehemiah 4:10). Nehemiah then brought more people to help out so that the laborers do not feel down as their health declines.

The soul, body, and spirit compile one being in man, and for him to defeat the despair that attacks the soul, he must have a strong spirit through prayer and faith, and he must also take care of his body in a healthy manner.

6. Nehemiah had sound vision and planning. The Holy Bible has a beautiful verse: "Where there is no revelation, the people cast off restraint" (Proverbs 29:18). Sometimes we interpret the word vision as looking ahead and a sound way of planning ahead, which is good, but that is not the true meaning. The word vision is a revelation from God that He wants me

to relay to others. The man who has a sound vision and wise planning is one to whom God reveals His will, and man is not able to receive that except by his personal relationship with God. If I am approaching a situation that is causing me to despair, I must ask, "What would God like me to do in this situation that is causing me to feel down?"

7. Nehemiah was organized and he broke up his effort so as to not deteriorate his energy; when every person works on the stone in front of his own house, then it is possible for a wall that is complete and sturdy to be built. So man must work in an organized manner in order to overcome failure and hopelessness: "For God is not the author of confusion but of peace, as in all the churches of the saints" (1 Corinthians 14:33). There was a problem that could have had an effect of helplessness on the disciples. They needed to figure out how to feed five thousand men plus women and children, making the total about twenty thousand people. They did not have anything but five loaves and two fish, and they said that even two hundred dinarii worth of food would not be enough for everyone to

have a meal. But our Lord Jesus Christ told the disciples to make the people sit down in groups of fifty, for order is very important. Nehemiah needed to pass out responsibilities to the people, so he made leaders over ten, leaders over fifty, and leaders over a thousand. He shared with them the work and did not place the burden only on himself.

Man must share with others when he faces a problem that may lead him to despair. Christ shared with His disciples; He gave them the food and the disciples gave it to the multitude. Nehemiah was able to have everyone work in harmony and unified their efforts so that their productivity may be great, and he instilled in them a team spirit and love and cooperation. He took advantage of the time in a good and an organized way, because time management is extremely important. A student who has many courses will feel despair if he wastes his time overthinking, but if he organizes his time and makes progress, he will succeed.

8. Nehemiah did not limit his job to just giving others commands, but he shared in the work and provided

the people with an example to follow. He also believed in encouragement and support. He put the people in groups that strengthened one another: "Therefore I positioned men behind the lower parts of the wall, at the openings; and I set the people according to their families, with their swords, their spears, and their bows" (Nehemiah 4:13). Nehemiah himself encouraged the men with words that weeded out fear from them and allowed them to not feel despair: "And I looked, and arose and said to the nobles, to the leaders, and to the rest of the people, 'Do not be afraid of them. Remember the Lord, great and awesome, and fight for your brethren, your sons, your daughters, your wives, and your houses'" (Nehemiah 4:14). Words of encouragement grant strength, and for this reason we must always encourage our children, so that they may defeat any failure or hopelessness. The book of Proverbs says, "The generous soul will be made rich, and he who waters will also be watered himself" (Proverbs 11:25). He who is watered will water others with words of encouragement, and in turn he will receive the same support from others.

9. One of the things that helped Nehemiah to defeat despair was remembering the goodness and promises

of God: "And I looked, and arose and said to the nobles, to the leaders, and to the rest of the people, "Do not be afraid of them. Remember the Lord, great and awesome" (Nehemiah 4:14). And this is the very thing that Saint Paul tells us: "Be anxious for nothing, but in everything by prayer and supplication, with thanksgiving, let your requests be made known to God; and the peace of God, which surpasses all understanding, will guard your hearts and minds through Christ Jesus" (Philippians 4:6–7).

10. When a person feels responsibility toward others and puts them before himself, he becomes motivated. For example, if a father and mother feel that their children are in danger, they let go of any feeling of despair and are charged to help their children even until death. This is what Nehemiah did and said: "and fight for your brethren, your sons, your daughters, your wives, and your houses" (Nehemiah 4:14). He told them that they are not fighting for their own sakes but for the sake of their brethren, sons, daughters, wives, and houses, and that those people they were fighting for have hope

in them, and told them to fight for their sakes. He encouraged them to do the work with enthusiasm.

> "I say to each one in a trial to say these three phrases: everything is for the good; it will soon end; God is present."

— His Holiness Pope Shenouda III —

11. When a person compares his experiences with those of others, he realizes that others have it worse than him, so it encourages him to keep going and not allow himself to fail, and he endures the hardships. This is what Nehemiah showed as well: "Those who built on the wall, and those who carried burdens, loaded themselves so that with one hand they worked at construction, and with the other held a weapon" (Nehemiah 4:17). When the nation saw the workers building with one hand and holding a weapon with the other hand, they stopped complaining, shook off their laziness, and also started working.

When a person looks to his own experience only, he sees that it is extremely difficult, so he is struck with despair. But when he looks at the experiences of others as well, he might become more encouraged. A problem took place between a couple, and the matter worsened to the point where it almost destroyed their relationship. After a few days, another family that they knew from church got into an accident, and it inspired the couple to ask themselves what the root of the disagreement is, finding it to be miniscule. They decided to reconcile, and decided to now live in peace.

I should not only look to the hardships of others in order to bear my own trials, but I should help them if I have the ability to. Nehemiah made the laborers work with one hand and hold weapons with the other.

What is the weapon that grants us victory against failure and despair? It is the word of God. As long as a person carries the word of God, it encourages him, comforts him, and gets him out of the feeling of despair: "God is our refuge and strength, a very present help in trouble. Therefore we will not fear, even though the earth be removed, and though the mountains be carried into the midst of the sea; though its waters roar and be troubled, though the mountains shake with its swelling" (Psalm 46:1–3).

Finally, we must trust that God has amazing plans for our lives, and therefore we will not allow for any situation to deprive us of enjoying life with God, even if we do not see His plans. And instead of surrendering to despair, our confidence in God must never cease, for His mercy is new every morning and what awaits us tomorrow is better than yesterday. Jeremiah the prophet says, "Through the Lord's mercies we are not consumed, because His compassions fail not. They are new every morning; great is Your faithfulness" (Lamentations 3:22–23).

3

SOME BIBLE VERSES FOR OVERCOMING HOPELESSNESS AND DESPAIR

"In the day when I cried out, You answered me, and made me bold with strength in my soul" (Psalm 138:3).

"The Lord also will be a refuge for the oppressed, a refuge in times of trouble" (Psalm 9:9).

"For thus says the high and lofty One Who inhabits eternity, whose name is Holy: 'I dwell in the high and holy place, with him who has a contrite and humble spirit, to revive the spirit of the humble, and to revive the heart of the contrite ones'" (Isaiah 57:15).

"Because he has set his love upon Me, therefore I will deliver him; I will set him on high, because he has known My name. He shall call upon Me, and I will answer him; I will be with him in trouble; I will deliver him and honor him. With long life I will satisfy him, and show him My salvation." (Psalm 91:14–16).

"And not only that, but we also glory in tribulations, knowing that tribulation produces perseverance; and perseverance, character; and character, hope. Now hope does not disappoint, because the love of God has been poured out in our hearts by the Holy Spirit who was given to us" (Romans 5:3–5).

www.ingramcontent.com/pod-product-compliance
Lightning Source LLC
Chambersburg PA
CBHW020954030426
42339CB00004B/95